FIGHTING
STRATEGY
WINNING COMBINATIONS

FIGHTING STRATEGY
WINNING COMBINATIONS

By Tom Schlesinger

DISCLAIMER

Please note that the publisher of this instructional book is NOT RESPONSIBLE in any manner whatsoever for any injury which may occur by reading and/or following the instructions herein.

It is essential that before following any of the activities, physical or otherwise, herein described, the reader or readers should first consult his or her physician for advice on whether or not the reader or readers should embark on the physical activity described herein. Since the physical activities described herein may be too sophisticated in nature, *it is essential that a physician be consulted.*

UNIQUE PUBLICATIONS

7011 SUNSET BLVD., HOLLYWOOD, CALIF. 90028-7597

© **UNIQUE PUBLICATIONS, INC., 1982**
All rights reserved
Printed in the United States of America

ISBN: 0-86568-035-3
Library of Congress No.: 82-70680

34567890□86 85 84 83

Design and layout Jeff Dungfelder

Editor. Daniel M. Furuya

DEDICATION

This book is dedicated to the two most important people in my life. To Alix Wolcott, whose unending love has taught me so much about life. Thank you for your patience.

Love, Tom

And to my stepson, Frank Endert, whom I love very much. Remember that in life all we can do is try. But when we try, we must know that we have tried to do the best we can. When you do anything less, you have only cheated yourself.

Love, Dad

ACKNOWLEDGEMENTS

You never get to this point in your life without the help of a lot of people. I would like to take this time to acknowledge just a few of the many people that have been an important part of my life.

To my mother, Betty Schlesinger, for her lifetime of love and understanding.

To my best friend and partner, Steve LaBounty who always makes me smile.

To my former wife, Bea Schlesinger. Thanks for a lot of good years.

To Harold Griffiths, for being such a good friend.

To Russell Rowe, for your assistance as my partner in the photos of this book.

And to all of those that have touched my life, and played such an important role in my development.

TABLE OF CONTENTS

BIOGRAPHY

Tom Schlesinger began his training in the martial arts in October of 1964. A friend was involved in training at a local karate school and asked Tom if he would like to come watch a class. Having little knowledge of the sport, he decided that it might be fun to see what it was all about. Little did Tom know that this innocent decision to accompany his friend would play such an important role in his life. After watching the class, Tom found himself intrigued with the athletic ability of the students. He approached the instructor and asked if he could be allowed to join the class. That was seventeen years ago, and this book is a result of that decision. The first seven years of his training was in the art of Goju-Kai Karate under the instruction of Rodney Hu. In the fall of 1967, Mr. Schlesinger received his black belt in Goju-Kai. He was tested for this rank by Gosei Yamaguchi, the head of Goju-Kai in the United States, and the son of Gogen "The Cat" Yamaguchi, tenth degree black belt and chief instructor of the Goju-Kai Karate Association in Japan. In his seventh year of training, his instructor suffered a back injury and was forced to temporarily close his school.

It was at this point that Tom decided to change styles from Goju-Kai Karate to Renbukai under the instruction of Ron Marchini. The change in styles was brought about by two factors. First, was the injury to his instructor. Secondly, Tom has always had an interest in competition; and in the Goju system, tournament fighting was strongly discouraged. By the fact that Ron Marchini was rated as the number one fighter in the country for two years in a row, Tom made the switch. For the next five years, Tom trained and eventually taught this system. During this time, he was made operations manager for the five Renbukai Schools in Northern California. In the winter of 1977, Tom received the rank of second degree black belt from the Renbukai Karate Association in Japan. In April of 1978, Tom decided that he was no longer interested in teaching karate for someone else on a full time basis and left the Marchini schools to start a new career.

In May of that same year, Tom was hired by Transamerica Title Insurance Company and has worked for the same company ever since. Originally hired as a business development officer, in less than two and one-half years, Tom had been promoted to county manager, in charge of operation for San Joaquin County.

Shortly after leaving the Renbukai Association, it became clear to Tom that he could not quit karate after all of these years. Several students had contacted him and asked if he was planning to open his own school. Since that time, he has taught classes two nights a week at Schlesinger's Renbukai Karate in Stockton, California. His school has 5000 square feet of training area and currently has eighty active students.

During his seventeen years of training, Tom has been involved with many different aspects of the art. Below is a list of his accomplishments.

TOURNAMENTS

During his nine years of tournament competition, Mr. Schlesinger won thirty-five trophies in individual freestyle, team freestyle, and kata. His most memorable competition was the last tournament, when, in 1973, he was the team captain at the North–South Karate Championships. One of the members of his team is the current Lightweight World Full-Contact Karate Champion, Benny Urquidez. The team took first place. Tom often says that he can't think of a better way to end his competitive career.

OFFICIATING

In the controversial world of officiating, Tom rose to become one of the most sought after referees in the United States. He has flown to many major tournaments strictly for the purpose of officiating the black belt finals. In the area of full-contact karate, Tom has been seen on national television officiating seven world title fights with competitors like Howard Jackson, Benny Urquidez, and Don Wilson. As a leader in the country on the subject of rules, Tom has authored the Schlesinger's Rule System, which is a comprehensive twenty-eight page rules booklet governing open competition.

TOURNAMENT PROMOTION

Tom is the co-promoter of the California State Karate Championships and Superstar National Karate Championships with his partner Steve LaBounty. This tournament has grown to become one of the most prestigious tournaments in the nation. This event has drawn the top fighters from all over the country who in 1981 fought for a record $7,000 in prize money. This was the largest cash purse ever offered to semi-contact fighters. This tournament was also the birthplace of such innovations as the open or creative kata. This division of musical katas with the use of gymnastics has quickly become one of the more popular aspects of the sport throughout the country. Many national tournaments have been literally stopped by standing ovations during the performance of an open kata competitor.

GENERAL

Tom has been featured in several of the national karate magazines over the past eight years, and has also appeared on the cover of *Karate Illustrated*. He was also listed as one of the top one hundred contributors to the growth of the martial arts in the book, "*WHO'S WHO IN KARATE*," written by Bob Wall. Tom is also a fight coordinator and has done stunt work in the motion picture, "*DEATH MACHINES*."

INTRODUCTION

When first asked to write a book, I spent many hours trying to determine what phase of the art would be the most beneficial to teach the reader. I couldn't decide on a topic. Would the basics be my choice or should I write about the value of kata in the martial arts? So many books have previously illustrated the basic techniques used in the various styles that writing another, I thought, would only be a duplication of already excellent efforts. To do a book on kata would be simple enough, during my seventeen years of training, I had learned over thirty forms in the styles of Goju-Kai, Renbukai, and Shotokan Karate. As time passed, however, I decided against this. Although the kata is a very critical part of every martial artist's training program, I felt that I could not convey the true spirit of a form through photos in a book. Finally, the search for a topic was ended. One night during a class that I was teaching, one of my intermediate students asked what was the most difficult thing I had learned in my years as a black belt. Without hesitation, I said that the most difficult material for me to grasp was freestyle strategies. My project began.

When I think back to when I first started my training, I have vivid recollections of how difficult it was just to learn my basic techniques. The hundreds of hours of training and the thousands of repetitions required just to learn the fundamental movements of the art. I can still remember how sore my legs felt after my first class. After all of the stretching and kicking we did that evening, the hardest thing I had to learn at that point was how to walk up the stairs for my second class. Just about the time my basics began to show progress and I was beginning to feel a little more confident in myself, my instructor asked me to move my feet while I executed my techniques. Move forward, move backward, move from side to side, block, counter punch, kick, this was harder than trying to chew gum and walk at the same time. Who did this guy think he was teaching? Then, he tells me to "focus" my technique and I don't even own a camera. Nothing could be harder than learning the basics. "Tonight, class, we will learn the art of the kata." Why, at eighteen years of age, do I have to learn how to go to the bathroom? If only it had been that simple. "Turn to the left, down block, lunge punch, step and turn, down block, lunge punch, front kick, back stance, chop block." If that wasn't bad enough, he then tells me to remember the sequence of these moves so I can perform them again next week. Then came the final challenge. "You better remember all of this material because you will be tested on it." Well, after four years and several tests, the big day came at last.

As a black belt, I realized that many new challenges awaited me. In looking back, I realize that my first challenge was getting my head through the door. Like most young black belts I had placed far too much importance on my rank. But like all other things, in time, this changed.

During the next few years of training, my katas began to show some improvement and my freestyle technique was also getting stronger. Yet, I felt there was still something missing in my kumite (sparring). There seemed to be a gap between the basic execution of my techniques and my ability to do freestyle. For months, I was unable to detect what I was missing in my training. "Was it my timing or did I need to develop a stronger mental attitude?" I wondered if I would ever find the missing piece to the puzzle. Then, as so often is the case, it was time for the instructor to learn from his student. While teaching a class, I was asked by one of my green belts what I thought would be the best techniques to use when initiating an attack on an opponent. I couldn't give my student an answer. Not that I hadn't been taught what techniques to start my attack with, but I wasn't sure that what I had learned was right. As a student, I had spent many hours practicing my opening moves, but no one had really explained why we use those particular techniques to start the attack. Then came the question of why we stood in a long front stance when we freestyled. It was at this moment that I realized I was teaching my students to stand that way because it was the way I had been taught by my instructor. None of these ideas had ever been challenged. It was always, "this is the way we do it in this style." So now I realized that everything I had learned up to that point was too mechanical. My instructors may have been 100% right in the material they were teaching me, but without teaching me the strategy of why we stood a particular way or why we throw our wheel kick in a certain manner, I could not function as a complete martial artist.

The next two years of my training was spent trying to understand the *strategies* of freestyle. This bridged the gap between my fighting and my basics. I began to question everything that I had learned. I never doubted the validity of the material I had been taught but now it was time for me to understand for myself the purpose and application of the techniques and theories I had learned over the past several years. I started with the basic stances. I began to analyze the strengths and weaknesses of each of the stances as well as formulate concepts of my own as to what constitutes a good fighting stance. From the stances, I began to question my ability and method of attacking my opponent. What was my objective in closing the distance and what lead techniques would best fulfill those objectives? Once the attack had begun and the distance had been closed, much thought had to be given to the types of combinations that could be thrown from these lead techniques. How could these techniques be used to create an opening on my opponent and allow me to score a point? Then came the question of defensive fighting. On the defensive, how could I get my opponent to make a mistake? Could I develop my blocks into effective weapons?

These are the questions I began to ask myself. The content of this book consists of the answers I have found. This book is directed to all students of the art who are still trying to bridge the gap between the basics and freestyle. I have especially written this book for those students that have the courage to ask, "why?"

CHAPTER I

STANCES

The stance selected by a student is the very foundation upon which he or she bases their ability to defend themselves. The selection of a stance will determine the type of techniques the individual will throw, the amount of power they will generate, and the amount and type of movement they will incorporate into their fighting techniques. Over the years, I have found that many students severely limit their freestyle fighting because of their lack of understanding of the strengths and weaknesses of the fighting stance they have selected or were taught. It is important that students fully understand the advantages and disadvantages of these stances and select the ones that are best suited for their own style of fighting.

It has always been my opinion that a good fighting stance should contain the three elements of flexibility, mobility, and stability. By flexibility, I mean that a student should be able to throw all of their techniques from one stance. If you watch an individual's freestyle, you will notice that many students change their stance to deliver various kicking techniques. For example, a competitor in a traditional front-stance may switch to a horse stance to throw a skipping-back-kick. Or, they may have to shorten their stance to throw an effective kick off the front leg. On the other hand, a competitor in a horse stance might switch to a front stance to obtain more use out of the rear leg. The point is that, when you make these changes in your stance, a good defensive fighter will be able to better anticipate the type of technique you are about to throw. With this anticipation, your opponent will have a better opportunity to avoid your attack and counter effectively. However, if you are able to deliver all of your techniques from the same stance, it will be much more difficult for your opponent to plan his defense. Although the opponent will realize that you have started your attack, it will become much more difficult for him to defend himself. He can never tell what technique you are going to use.

Mobility in a fighting stance gives the student the ability to move quickly in any direction. Movement in a stance is a weapon in itself. The best illustration of how movement can set the pattern of a fight was the second match between Roberto Duran and Sugar Ray Leonard. Roberto Duran is considered to be one of the most aggressive and punishing fighters ever to step into the ring. But, on the night of November 25, 1980, the ability of Leonard to move in the ring was more than Duran could handle. For seven and one-half rounds, Leonard was able to evade the relentless attacks of the champion from Panama and recapture the world title from the same man that beat him only a few months earlier when Leonard tried to fight toe-to-toe with Duran.

Stability in a fighting stance means that your stance must be strong enough to withstand the charge of your opponent. Although Sugar Ray was able to avoid the charge of the champion for most of the fight, there were several occasions when Duran was successful in closing the distance and unloaded some savage combinations on his opponent. Because of Leonard's ability to maintain a strong fighting stance, he was able to maintain good body positioning and counter-punch effectively throughout the fight. If Leonard's movement put him in an awkward position at the moment of Duran's attack, the results of the fight might have been quite different. The important thing to remember is that you must be able to maintain a good stance whenever you move. Many students will start in a good fighting stance but, once they begin to move around, they change the position of their feet causing their stance to become very weak.

In this chapter, we will explore the advantages and disadvantages of the most commonly used fighting stances. Study them well for they will play an important role in developing your own ability to fight both offensively and defensively.

Front Stance

This traditional fighting stance is still used today by many of the Japanese and Okinawan styles of karate. The weight distribution will vary from sixty percent on the front leg and forty percent on the back leg to seventy percent on the front leg and thirty percent on the back leg, depending on the style of karate you are practicing. As mentioned earlier, the stance you select will determine the type of techniques you will be able to throw, the power you will be able to generate, and the amount of movement you will be able to incorporate into your fighting. This statement is clearly illustrated when you examine the strengths and weaknesses of this stance.

One of the advantages of this stance, as you can see in the photos, is that, with its long, low posture, it offers the fighter a great deal of power and stability. If you have ever seen a traditional Japanese style tournament, you will note that the fighters are very secure in their stance and concentrate mainly on power techniques. You will also notice that the fighter that utilizes this type of stance normally depends a great deal on powerful punching techniques with either hand. The effectiveness of their hand techniques is, in part, created by the fact that their body faces directly towards their opponent. This body position offers the competitor a wide variety of both offensive and defensive hand techniques from which to select. Much of the strength they generate in their punching comes from the low center of gravity in their stance and their ability to use their hips and legs to add power to their punching techniques. When it comes to leg techniques, the Japanese and Okinawan style fighters are considered to have powerful rear leg attacks, with the utilization of both kicking and sweeping techniques. The dominance of rear leg techniques can be attributed to the fact that, with the majority of the weight being placed on the front leg, the back leg is free to attack.

As in any fighting stance, this also has its disadvantages. The first problem is that, when you put yourself in this lower, stronger position to fight, you limit your ability to move. In watching these students compete with each other, you will notice that they are very rigid in their fighting with only minimal movement straight forwards and backwards. When competing with an individual that moves a great deal, these students often will have trouble in closing the distance.

Facing your opponent can offer some advantages offensively as well as create some problems defensively. If you examine the frontal view of this stance at the beginning of this section, you will notice that this forward position leaves your body and head open for attack from many different angles. This necessitates that, if you select this stance, you must become very proficient in your defensive blocking and distancing skills. Another disadvantage is in the weight distribution of this stance. With the majority of the weight placed on the front leg, it becomes difficult to use this leg for either offensive or defensive kicking. Without the use of the front leg, you have one less weapon against your opponent.

Look at some illustrations of these strengths and weaknesses so you will better understand how your stance affects the type of technique you can execute.

Front view.

Side view.

Traditional Front Stance (advantage)

Without a doubt, the biggest advantage of the traditional front stance is the strong base it gives the competitor. The low center of gravity and the ability of the students to rotate their hips into the punch lends itself to powerful techniques. In this example, you can see that as the attacker starts his round-house-kick, the defender makes no effort to move backwards. Because of the strong foundation of this stance, the defender is able to block this attack without being knocked off balance. From here, he is in a position to deliver a powerful reverse-punch which drives his opponent off balance. Once his opponent is driven backwards the defender can continue with a powerful front-kick from the rear leg which will continue to keep his opponent on the defensive. This is an example of the type of power techniques that you will typically see thrown by fighters using a traditional front stance.

Fighting stance.

Wheel kick.

Reverse punch.

Front kick.

Traditional Front Stance (disadvantage)

Like all stances this one also has its disadvantages. Because of its long base and low center of gravity, this stance offers the fighter limited mobility and makes it difficult to kick with the front leg. In this illustration, you can clearly see how this stance creates this problem. If a fighter, using this stance, wanted to kick with the front leg, he would first have to shift his rear leg forward so he could lift his front leg for the kick, without losing his balance. This extra step will often alert and telegraph to your opponent that you are about to attack. As we have shown in this series of photos, by the time the attacker delivers his kick, his opponent has moved easily out of range. A lead kick from the front leg, when using this stance, will usually be wasted and ineffective. If you watch a traditional tournament where this stance is frequently used, you will notice that the competitors seldom, if ever, kick with their front leg.

Fighting stance.

Advancing on the opponent.

Starting the kick.

Execution—the kick short of the target.

Traditional Horse Stance

This version of the horse stance is used in some Okinawan styles as well as many Korean and kempo forms of karate. The weight distribution of this stance is fifty percent of your weight on each leg. From time to time, you will see some competitors putting more weight on the back leg in order to free their front leg for defensive kicking. One of the advantages in selecting this stance is the fact that it offers the student a good defensive posture. If you examine the illustration of this stance, you will notice that, as the opponent, you will see very few openings with which to start your attack. This is contrary to the front stance which will offer several openings to choose. In addition to being a good defensive fighting position, this stance also offers a great deal of stability to the competitor. As in the traditional front stance, the low center of gravity gives this stance a powerful base from which to operate.

Another advantage of this stance is created by its wide base. With the feet spread apart, the student has the ability to shift his weight to the rear leg increasing the distance between him and his opponent. This gives the individual the extra time and distance to score with a defensive side kick. In watching students who fight from this stance, you will note that this technique is used quite often.

One of the major disadvantages of this stance is created by the angle of your body. By being turned sideways to your opponent, it is often difficult to generate defensive punching power. This loss of power is created by the student's inability to rotate their hips into the technique. This rotation is what creates the extra power for the punch. Although the students have the option to move their front leg to the side, which would give them the ability to rotate their hips with their punch, this theory is very seldom applied. If you examine fighters who use the traditional horse stance, you will notice that the vast majority of these individuals continue to punch across their body when striking defensively with the rear hand.

Kicking with the rear leg is another example of the problems with this stance. Although you can kick from the rear leg in this stance, the problem arises from the fact that you must first turn your hips toward your opponent before executing the technique. This additional movement will often telegraph your attack, allowing your opponent the time to retreat and avoid your technique.

Let us now examine the strengths and weaknesses of this stance through the following illustrations.

Front view.

Side view.

Traditional Horse Stance (advantage)

Because of the wide base of this stance, the competitor has the ability to quickly shift all of his weight to his rear leg. This weight shift will create a distancing problem for the attacker. As the defender shifts his weight to the rear leg, his head and body move back a considerable distance. This extra distance will cause the attacker's first technique to be useless and will force him to take an additional step towards the defender in order to score with a second or counter technique. It is during this step that the defender has the best opportunity to counter. As the defender shifts his weight, he has cocked his leg into a defensive kicking position. From this position, he waits for the attacker to continue his combination. As his opponent takes another step forward to deliver his second punch, the defender executes a defensive side kick and the attacker runs into the full power of the counter.

Fighting stance.

Step across—reverse punch.

Second reverse punch.

Defensive side kick.

Traditional Horse Stance (disadvantage)

The major weakness of this stance lies in the inability of its practitioners to turn their hips into the opponent when countering the punch. As I mentioned earlier, the student using this stance has the capability to rotate their hips towards their opponent and increase the power of their counter. Over the years, it has been my experience that this seldom occurs. Students using this stance often throw their defensive punch across their body losing a great deal of power. In this illustration, you will see how this loss of power can put you at a distinct disadvantage. As the attacker throws his lead technique, the defender counters with a reverse-punch that is delivered across his body. Even though this technique strikes the attacker, it does not have the power or focus necessary to stop his momentum. This allows the offensive fighter to continue his attack and maintain control over the defender.

Fighting stance.

Reverse punch.

Counter across the body.

Attacker maintaining control.

Cat Stance

The cat stance is most often used by the students of Goju-Kai Karate. The weight distribution of this stance calls for ninety percent of the weight to be placed on the back leg, while only ten percent of the body weight rests on the front leg. The major advantage of this stance is that, with only ten percent of the fighter's weight placed on the front leg, it can be used for quick defensive kicking.

Having studied Goju-Kai for seven years, I have personally found several weaknesses in this stance. This stance offers little flexibility and range of techniques for the student. With ninety percent of the weight placed on the back leg, it is impossible to kick with the rear leg without first redistributing the weight to the front leg. This extra step takes time and will alert the defender that you are about to attack. The end result is that your opponent is often moving out of the range of your attack with no advantage being gained to yourself.

The second major problem that I found with the cat stance is in its stability. If you look at a side view of this stance, you will notice that the feet are placed close together. Because of this narrow base, it is difficult to execute your hand techniques with power. As with the kicks, in order to punch with power, you must first move your front foot forward. It is my experience that students using this stance are often caught off guard when attacked. If you could close the distance on your opponent in this stance, before he had a chance to react, you could catch him in this stance. This would make it difficult for him to exchange punches effectively.

Let us look at a few illustrations that might better clarify your understanding of this stance.

Front view.

Side view.

Cat Stance (advantage)

As I have mentioned before, the major advantage of this stance is the ability of the student to kick with the front leg. This can be very helpful when you are attacked and forced into a defensive position. When your opponent begins their lead technique, it is important that, as the defender, you start your counter immediately. In this illustration, you will see that as soon as the attacker starts his movement, the defender's front leg also initiates its movement. As the attacker extends his lead punch, the defender executes a defensive front kick to the body. Once the defender has stopped the charge of his opponent, he will now move out of the cat stance and begin his attack. In this particular illustration, I use a reverse-punch to the body.

Fighting stance.

Attack—beginning defense.

Defensive front kick.

Reverse punch.

Cat Stance (disadvantage)

An interesting point that must be made in regards to this stance, is its major advantage that can also at the same time prove to be a major disadvantage. Like any defensive technique, the successful execution of the kick is based on proper distancing and timing. In this illustration, you will see one of the problems that can be created when your opponent breaks your timing. As the attacker begins his lead move, the defender begins to raise his leg for his defensive kick. You will notice, in this example, the offensive fighter has closed a great deal of distance on his lead move. When the defender tries to execute his front kick, he finds that the attacker is too close jamming his kick. As the attacker continues with his forward momentum, he catches the defender with one leg in the air and easily drives him backwards. In this example, the offensive fighter continues his attack with a reverse punch. The point should be made that, whenever you try to kick off the front leg in this manner, you run the risk of being jammed by your opponent and driven from your stance.

Fighting stance.

Lead backhand.

Defender jammed.

Reverse punch.

Modified Horse Stance

With the development and evolution of karate in the United States, there has been a great deal of change and modification in the traditional arts. Some of the changes have been very constructive and have served to broaden the ability of the martial artist. On the other hand, some of the changes that have taken place in this country have set the science of fighting back many years. The next two stances we will discuss have their roots here in the United States. These are two of the more constructive changes developed in this country.

The modified horse stance is nothing more than a modified traditional horse stance. By shortening the base of the stance, it has become far more effective in freestyle fighting. The traditional horse stance, while being very strong and stable, lacked mobility and flexibility. When watching two students fight from a traditional horse stance, you find that neither fighter used much movement in their stances. Seldom would you see a kick thrown with the rear leg. With the shortening of this stance, today's fighters have become very mobile. It is a rare sight, these days, to see two fighters set in their stances waiting for the other to move. Movement has become a critical part of a fighter's arsenal. This narrower base in the stance has also greatly increased the ability of the student to kick with the rear leg. Although students using this stance will still have to turn their hips as they kick with the rear leg, they are now able to execute this movement with greater ease.

The modification of this stance has left the student with one major weakness. With its shorter base, the fighter will lose some of the stability offered by the traditional stance. This loss of stability can create problems for the fighter who is being attacked.

Front view.

Side view.

Modified Horse Stance (advantage)

The modification of this stance has given today's fighter a greater capacity for movement and a wider variety of both offensive and defensive techniques from which to select. This series of photos will illustrate the flexibility gained by the use of this stance. The shorter base now allows the student to kick from the front leg without having to take any additional steps. In this sequence, the attacker leads with a wheel-kick to the groin. As the defender reacts with a block, his opponent continues the attack with a quick back-hand to the head, followed by a reverse-punch to the body. Now that the attacker has driven his opponent out of his stance, he can continue his attack with the use of a front-kick as we have shown. This is a very explosive four-part combination that can be utilized from this stance. If you try this combination from a traditional horse stance, you will find it very difficult to execute this technique. This illustrates the new versatility that has been given to the fighter with the modification of this stance.

Fighting stance.

Attack begins.

Wheel kick to the groin.

Backhand.

Reverse punch.

Front kick.

Modified Horse Stance (disadvantage)

Anytime you put yourself in a higher stance, you lose some of your stability and may find it difficult to stop a fighter who has a strong charge. It has been my experience that the shortened stance creates a loss of punching power. This loss of power forces many students to attempt a defensive kick to stop the attack of their opponent. If the timing of this kick is not perfect, you may find yourself in this type of situation. As the attacker closes the distance, the defender lifts his leg to prepare for his kick. By the time his leg is in position, his opponent has already jammed the attempted counter. Now the defender is up on one leg and is in serious trouble. With the defender caught in this weakened position, the attacker is able to grab his opponent and take complete physical control. As long as the attacker is able to maintain this control, he will be able to continue with his combination and keep the other fighter on the defensive.

Fighting stance.

Attack begins.

Defender jammed.

Attacker takes control.

Reverse punch.

Wheel kick.

Modified Front Stance

The modification of the front stance has brought about the same type of change as the modified horse stance. The shortening of this stance has given the student a far wider range of techniques to throw and has added a great deal of movement to the matches. It should be pointed out, at this time, that this extra movement has placed an increasing demand on the students. Knowing how to move properly has become a totally new aspect of the art. This concept of movement and the problems it can create for the fighter will be discussed in later chapters.

The modification of this stance has also brought about a change in the weight distribution. In a modified front stance, the weight is evenly distributed with fifty percent on each leg. Remember that, in the traditional front stance, the weight distribution had sixty percent of the weight on the front leg. This change has made it possible for students using this stance, to throw a wider variety of kicking techniques that could not be executed from the traditional one.

Just as in the case of the horse stance, some of the stability of this stance has been lost with this modification. But with the additional flexibility and mobility you gain in this stance, it is often worth the risk.

Front view.

Side view.

Modified Front Stance (advantages)

For years, fighters that used the traditional front stance were known for their powerful punching and their strong front kicks from the rear leg. Seldom, if ever, would this fighter attempt to kick from the front leg or spin around to execute a technique. To this day, many traditional styles argue that techniques of this nature are of no value and have no power. In this illustration, you will see an example of how this modified front stance has given the fighter the capability to throw a wider variety of techniques. As the defender blocks the lead wheel-kick of his opponent, notice that his hips are already beginning to turn with the motion of the block. Once the attack has been blocked, the defender continues this rotation. Lifting his leg as he spins, the defender executes a spinning heel-kick to the head of his opponent. This is a technique that could not be thrown from the traditional front stance. But, with the modification of this stance, students now have the option to throw this type of technique.

Fighting stance.

Left wheel kick.

Defender starting to spin.

Spinning wheel kick.

Modified Front Stance (disadvantage)

Having trained in the traditional Japanese styles for several years, I can tell you that these styles base their entire fighting on the strength of their stance. And I will be the first to advise you that, if the foundation of your opponent is weak, you should attack the stance. With this modified stance, being higher than the traditional stance, you will find that you are more vulnerable to this type of attack. When your opponent is not in a strong stance, you can gain the advantage on the defender by attacking his front leg with a foot sweep. By kicking his leg out from under him, the defender's position can easily be weakened as we have illustrated. Once he is in this position, you will find it easy to score. In this example, I strike the defender with a reverse-punch. Just remember that when your center of gravity is high, you are vulnerable to this type of attack.

These are the most commonly used fighting stances today. No matter which stance you select, it will have its good and bad points. The key for you, the student, is to study the strengths and weaknesses of each of these stances. Plan your fighting style with these strengths and weaknesses in mind. And above all, if you are not happy with your foundation or stance, change it to a more suitable one.

Fighting stance.

Lead foot sweep.

Defender set off-balance.

Reverse punch.

A good fighting stance consists of:

1. Flexibility.

2. Mobility.

3. Stability.

A good stance determines:

1. The type of technique you can execute.

2. How much power you can generate.

3. Your ability to move.

CHAPTER II

CLOSING THE DISTANCE (LEAD TECHNIQUES)

In order to become an effective offensive fighter, the first thing a student must learn is how to close the distance on his opponent by the use of the proper lead technique. The student's selection of the proper lead technique will directly affect his ability to close the distance on his opponent. While most students have a large number of techniques in their arsenal, you will find through practice that many of these techniques are ineffective as a lead attack. That is not to say that the technique itself is poor, but only that it does not fulfill the requirements of being a good lead technique.

At this point, let's stop and define exactly what are the elements of a good lead technique. First, it must be a technique that allows you to close the distance quickly on your opponent. Secondly, the technique should place a weapon between you and the defender immediately. And finally, a good lead technique should create an opening on your opponent. But let us examine these three elements further, to better understand just what they mean, and how they should be applied to improve your freestyle fighting.

In order for a lead technique to close the distance quickly, two conditions must take place. The first is that the student must remember that the technique must lead the attack. What I mean by this is that the student must practice starting the technique, whether it is a punch or kick, first, and then have their body move after the technique is on its way to the target. If you watch students carefully, you will notice that the opposite usually happens. The attacker will move his body towards the opponent first and then try to deliver a technique once this motion has been started. This movement will create two problems with your attack. The first problem is that, with your body moving towards your opponent before the technique is started, you are temporarily susceptible to a counter attack. This weakness is created because you are moving into the striking range of the defender without having started a technique of your own. (This concept will be illustrated in this chapter to clarify any confusion over this concept.) Secondly, by moving your body before you begin your attack, you have just telegraphed to your opponent that you are about to charge. This error will often give the defender enough warning to avoid your attack. This concept is especially important for students that are not blessed with blinding speed. By practicing this theory of starting the technique first before moving your body forward, you will find that the defending student will be deceived by the smoothness of your attack. They will not start to react to this movement until your technique is well under way. This smooth delivery will give them the impression that you are much faster than you really are. Remember, it is not that you are making your arms or legs move any faster during the attack, but it's that you are eliminating all of the wasted motion. This gives your opponent the impression of greater speed. In the attack, it is not important how fast you think you are moving, but how fast your opponent thinks you are moving. The second condition that creates a fast lead technique is that the technique should take the shortest route possible to the opponent. It should come as no surprise that the shortest route is a straight line.

The next element of a good lead technique is that it must place immediately a weapon between yourself and your opponent. I believe that this is a major problem for many students today. When attacking, they will continually select lead techniques that do not place a weapon between the opponent and themselves. For example, techniques like a spinning back kick, ridge hand, and wheel kick are not good lead techniques when you are attacking. These techniques, however, might make for an excellent follow-up move in your attack. I also recognize that many of these techniques can be used very effectively as a defensive counter. What we will try to illustrate in this chapter is that many of the techniques you have learned, although effective if used properly, are not the best choice for the first move of your attack.

To further illustrate this point, let's compare our art to boxing. Fighters in that sport, as in ours, learn a variety of combinations and punches to use with either hand. Yet, would you expect to see a top quality boxer start an attack with an uppercut? Many of them will not start their attack with a hook because it leaves them vulnerable to a counter attack. A vast majority of their lead moves consist of a left jab and a right cross. Both of these punches put a weapon between themselves and their opponent which makes them very effective lead techniques. You must remember that the main objective of a lead technique is to close the distance on your opponent quickly without giving him a chance to throw an effective counter. Once this distance between the two fighters has been reduced, you can then choose from a large number of techniques to throw while continuing your attack.

The final phase of a good lead technique is that it should create an opening on your opponent. There are two types of openings. The most recognizable is the active opening. Simply stated, this opening occurs when Fighter A attacks with a lead move. Fighter B, in an effort to defend against this attack, attempts a block which leaves another portion of his body open. Fighter A then continues his attack by scoring with a second technique to the opening which has just been created.

Another type of opening that is often created (but seldom recognized by the students) has to do with the fighting stance. As you will recall, we discussed the importance of a good fighting stance in the opening chapter. The stance plays an important role in the students' ability to defend themselves. When you throw your lead technique, you should learn to become aware of what your opponent is doing in regards to their fighting stance. If they are moving back and maintaining the same fighting stance, you have gained no additional advantage past the active opening you are attempting to create. However, if your lead technique is delivered quickly and with power, it will often force your opponent into a weaker fighting stance. This change will decrease the defending fighter's ability to counter and will give you an added advantage as the attacker. This type of opening is just as important as an active opening. You must learn to become aware of your opponent's stances and take advantage of their weaknesses whenever possible.

Now let's take a look at some illustrations of proper and improper lead techniques and the positive and negative effect these techniques may have on your freestyle fighting.

Spinning Back Kick (Improper Lead Technique)

This first technique clearly illustrates the problems that can be created by selecting the lead technique. Although the circle-back kick is a powerful technique, it should not be used as the opening move of your initial attack.

As the attack begins to develop, you will notice that this technique does not put a weapon (the foot) between the attacker and the opponent. This gives the defender the opportunity to move inside the attacker's lead. By the time the attacker extends his kick, the defender has already slipped inside and started his counter attack. At this point, the attacker now finds himself on the defensive and in a very dangerous position. As the action continues, you can see that the original defender has now gained total control of the situation and is on the attack. If the student had selected a better lead technique, he would not find himself in this situation.

Fighting stance.

Attacker starts—spinning back kick.

Kick misses.

Defender counters with a reverse punch.

Skipping Back Kick (Improper Lead Technique)

Although the skipping back kick can be a very effective lead move, many students throw this technique in such a fashion that it gets them into trouble.

If you look carefully, you will see that the attacking student has made a critical mistake. Although he has started to close the distance quickly and with a powerful lead technique, he has again failed to put a weapon between himself and his opponent. The attacker has lifted his leg in preparation for the kick, but his heel is pointing down to the floor and not at his opponent. This error gives the defender the opportunity to move inside and jam the kick before the attacker can raise his heel to the proper kicking position. Being caught in this position, the defender now has the additional problem of trying to defend himself while standing on one leg. Now that the defender is trapped in this position, he will find it almost impossible to stop the charge of his opponent. From this position, it will be an easy task for the attacker to continue his counter as we have illustrated. The proper execution of the skipping back-kick as a lead technique will be demonstrated later in this chapter.

Fighting stances.

Attacker starts a skipping back kick.

Defender jams the attack.

Follow-up reverse punch.

Ridge Hand (Improper Lead Technique)

The ridgehand technique in karate is equivalent to the hook in boxing. Although both are powerful techniques, neither should be used to start the attack. As the fighter begins his attack, you can clearly see how open he is for a counterattack. The ridgehand being a circular technique, forces the attacker to bring his arm outside of his body line to deliver the strike. This outside motion does not put a weapon between them and gives the defender a straight line to counter attack. Remember, the idea of a good lead technique is to put your opponent on the defensive both physically and mentally. By having this gap in your attack, you give the defender both the time and opportunity to plan for and execute his counter. In this sequence of photos, that is exactly what has taken place. The defender, seeing the opening, stops his opponent's charge with a straight right jab. Once the attack has been neutralized, the defender can continue his counter attack. In this situation, I have selected a reverse punch to the body for my follow-up technique.

Fighting stance.

Lead ridgehand.

Counter right jab.

Follow-up reverse punch.

Wheel Kick or Roundhouse Kick

The wheel kick off the front leg is probably the most misused lead technique in karate. If you go to a tournament, or watch students freestyle fight at a school, you will see hundreds of illustrations of the misuse of this technique. The problem with this technique as a lead attack is illustrated in this series of pictures. Although the knee of the attacker is high and pointed at his opponent, you will notice that the foot (the weapon) is pointing to the outside of the defender's body. This gives the defender the chance to move inside and jam the kick before it can be delivered. By jamming the kick at this point, you will once again catch your opponent with one leg in the air, making it very difficult for him to defend himself. This then gives you an excellent opportunity to counter his attack. In this series of pictures, the counter attack is a reverse punch. An exception to the rule is the former World Full-Contact Karate Champion, Bill Wallace. For years, Bill has been using a wheel kick off of the front leg to devastate his opponent. Without going into great detail at this point, let me say that this was due in part to Bill's ability to throw a variety of kicks from this one lead position. This concept will be discussed in the chapter entitled "Combinations From a Lead Technique."

Fighting stance.

Lead wheel kick.

Defender jams the attack.

Counter technique.

Front Kick

Although the front kick is an excellent lead technique, as you will see later in this chapter, I have chosen this technique to illustrate a common mistake made by many students. This error is not only made during the execution of this technique, but it occurs in many of the lead techniques used by fighters. This simple mistake has resulted in the attacking fighter being hit with a counter attack on many occasions. The attacker's mistake in this series of pictures is that he is taking a step forward before he starts his technique. Remember, one of the elements of a good lead technique is that the weapon moves first. This wind up, or short step, moves you into the defender's zone and allows him the opportunity to counter attack before you can start your own attack. This mistake is a common error among students of all ranks. You must pay close attention that your weapon moves first.

Now that we have seen some of the problems that are created by selecting the improper lead technique, let us now study those techniques that would be of better use when initiating the attack.

Fighting stance.

Lead jab.

Follow-up reverse punch.

Wheel kick to the head.

The Jab

There are two key points that you should be made aware of in the second picture. First you will notice that the jab has started to move before the body lunges forward. As we have discussed in this chapter, this will change your opponent's reaction time and give them the illusion of greater speed. The second point is that when you couple this speed of delivery with the concept of having the weapon between you and your opponent; the reaction of the defender will be defensive in nature rather than aggressive in a counter attack. That is exactly what has happened in this series of pictures. Rather than trying to counter attack, the defender must go on the defensive to block the jab. Once his opponent has begun this defensive move, the attacker may now throw a second technique and continue to keep the other fighter on the defensive. By now, the distance has been closed and the offensive fighter can choose from a number of techniques to continue his attack. One suggestion is a follow-up wheel kick to the head.

Fighting stance.

Attack begins.

Lead front kick.

Follow-up lunge punch.

Front Kick

As this attack begins to develop, you can clearly see that the weapon (the foot) is between the attacker and his opponent. The placement of the foot in this position stops the opponent from trying to move inside the technique and forces him to defend himself against the kick. As he begins his block to stop the kick, you will notice that the head is now open for attack. Once this opening is created, I will continue my attack with a lunge-punch to the head. You will notice that although we have concluded the attack with this technique, I am still in position to continue with any additional offensive techniques if necessary, to score on my opponent. If you examine the final picture in this sequence, you will see that I have maintained my fighting stance while, at the same time, driving my opponent into an awkward fighting position. This will make it increasingly difficult for my opponent to defend himself. Remember, we discussed the advantage you can gain by driving your opponent out of their stance. That advantage is illustrated in the last photo.

Fighting stance.

Attacker stepping forward beginning front kick.

Defender jams lead move.

Counter attack with a left reverse punch. Right hand strike to the head.

Back Hand

In this lead technique, we have the attacker starting from a modified horse stance. The attack begins with the fighter lunging forward with a backhand to close the distance. Again, note that the attacking hand is well in front of the body forcing the defender into a defensive position. Because of the explosive lead technique, the defender has been forced to raise his front arm in an effort to block this attack. At the same time this back hand is being thrown, the attacker shortens his stance in preparation for a follow-up technique. As the defender lifts his arm, I cock my leg and deliver a skipping-back-kick to this newly created opening. With my opponent being driven off balance from the power of this technique, I am now able to continue my attack with the technique of my choice. In this sequence, I finish the combination with a back hand to the head. The important thing for you to remember is that this combination cannot be effective without the lead technique setting the momentum of the charge.

Fighting stance.

Lead backhand.

Attacker adjusts stance.

Preparation for the follow-up.

Skipping back kick.

Backhand.

Skipping Back Kick

The skipping back kick can either be a good lead technique or it can get you into a lot of trouble. If you will refer back when we demonstrated the skipping back kick as an improper lead technique, we can compare the differences in delivery. In the illustration of the improper lead technique, you will notice two important points. First, the attacking fighter has leaped into the air in anticipation of his opponent moving back. This leaping motion takes extra time and gives the defender an opportunity to counter. Secondly, you will notice in the illustration of a poor lead technique, that the attacker has not yet cocked his leg into position to deliver the kick. Instead, his foot is pointing downward with the weapon aimed at the floor. In the example of a good lead technique, you will see just the opposite. The attacker has taken a shorter step towards his opponent, giving the defender less time to counter. Secondly, as the attacker advances, he has cocked his leg into the proper kicking position thus putting the weapon between himself and his opponent. These are the two important elements that make this skipping back kick a better lead technique than our previous example. After delivering the lead technique, I follow-up by stepping behind my opponent's lead leg. At this point, the follow-up technique will consist of a reverse leg takedown. To execute this technique, you kick the defender's leg out from under him while, at the same time, pulling his upper body in the opposite direction. Once the opponent is down, you may follow-up with the technique of your choice. Here, I use a punch to the head.

Fighting stance.

Attack begins.

Back kick scores.

Step behind lead leg.

Reverse leg takedown.

Follow-up.

Front Leg Wheel Kick to the Groin

As I mentioned earlier in this chapter, I don't feel that a front leg wheel kick is a good technique. I have found over the years that there is one exception to the rule. The wheel kick to the groin off the front leg is probably the fastest kicking technique a student can learn. The key factor to developing the speed to this technique is that the kicking leg must move first. In the illustration, you will notice that my leg is far in front of my body as I attack. As a student, you must train yourself to execute the kick in this fashion. As the kick is delivered, I have pushed off my back leg to close the distance on the other fighter. When practicing this movement, you should not have a jumping or hopping motion on the back leg. In pushing off the back leg, you should create a sliding motion on the front foot while moving forward. As the opening is created by my lead leg, I continue my attack with the use of a back hand to the head.

In concluding this chapter, there are several concepts that I want to repeat about closing the distance with a lead technique. They are important to remember. First, you must realize that one of the main purposes of a lead technique is to close the distance between yourself and the other fighter. Bridging the gap is important if you expect to be effective in your combination. If you can't close a major portion of the distance with the first technique, it will be difficult to score with the second. Secondly, it is important that you select a lead technique that places a weapon between yourself and your opponent. The importance of this concept lies in the fact that by placing the weapon between both of you, the defensive fighter will find it hard to initiate a counter attack. Learn to lead with techniques that attack your opponent on a direct, straight line. Once you have closed the distance with a lead move, you can continue your attack with a variety of punches or kicks. And finally, a good lead move should create an opening on your opponent. This can be either a physical opening, or a technical mistake such as causing your opponent to move into an awkward fighting stance. Learn to throw your first technique with a purpose in mind. Don't throw token techniques at the defender. If you are going to be the attacker, you must learn to make things happen when you move.

Fighting stance.

Attack begins.

Wheel kick to the groin.

Backhand to the head.

A good lead technique:

1. Allows you to close the distance on your opponent.

2. Keeps a weapon (hand or foot) between yourself and your opponent.

3. Creates an opening for attack.

CHAPTER III

COMBINATIONS FROM LEAD TECHNIQUES (KICKS)

Selecting the proper lead technique will play an important role in your ability to develop yourself as an offensive fighter. But using the proper lead movement is not the only key to success. It is important that you train yourself to throw a variety of combinations from the lead movement. The importance of developing good combinations from your initial attack lies in the fact that, as the aggressor, you will seldom score on your opponent with your first move. As the defender, the reaction is often to move back to avoid the first technique and then try to move in for a counter attack. This creates the need for effective combinations on the part of the offensive fighter, in order to keep his opponent on the defensive and at a disadvantage.

How many times have you watched a student either in class or at a tournament, lead with just one technique and then stop his attack? For those of you that are caught in this trap, let me pass along the results of a rather unscientific but revealing study that I did at my school. It is the purpose for having this chapter in my book. A few years ago, I took a group of students, twenty to be exact, paired them off with each other and gave them the following instructions. "As the aggressor you are allowed one technique which can be either a punch or a kick. Your goal is to try and close the distance on your opponent with this one technique, and score a point. The objective of the defender is to try and move out of the way once the attack has been started and avoid being hit." Each attacker was given ten chances to score a point with their opening move. The ten attackers had ten chances each. There was a possible one-hundred points that could possibly be scored. At the end of this test, we found that a total of only eighteen points were actually scored by the attacking contestants. Only eighteen percent of the total possible points, or less than one out of five lead techniques actually struck their opponent. This indicates that the initial attack was not at all effective in scoring a point We then modified the instructions and told the offensive fighter that they could now throw a second technique and were allowed to take a second step forward in order to close the distance on their opponent during the attack. The instructions remained the same for the defender and each attacker was given another ten chances. The final results of this test indicated that just over half, or fifty-two percent of the students, had scored with either their first or second technique. Almost three times as many points had been scored when the attacking student was allowed to throw an additional punch or kick. Finally, we gave the attacker the chance to throw a combination using three techniques. They were also allowed to take one additional step during the attack. They could now take a maximum of three steps forward in an attempt to catch the opponent. The defender was instructed to take only whatever evasive action was necessary to avoid being hit. Eighty-nine points were scored during this portion of the test. The students attacking with a three part combination were successful almost nine out of ten times. It should be pointed out that during this study, the defensive student was not given the opportunity to counter. We were merely trying to measure the effect of closing the distance with combinations as compared with one single technique used to score a point. The results indicated that a student could be almost five times as effective when they attack using three moves in their combination, instead of throwing one technique and stopping.

In this chapter, we will concentrate on a variety of combinations from one lead position. I will try to teach you a variety of techniques that can be thrown from your initial lead movement. The purpose of this theory is that when our opponent begins to defend against our lead move, we can change our angle of attack and make our opponent's defense useless. These combinations are very effective against the defender that tries to counter your lead attack by either blocking and countering, or distancing and countering. In the next chapter, we will discuss explosive hand combinations that can be used when your opponent is moving backwards a great deal to avoid your lead technique. A perfect example of the theory we will be discussing in this chapter is the kicking style of Bill Wallace, the former World Middleweight Full-Contact Karate Champion. Bill was always known as the fastest and most effective kicker in competition. It was this tremendous kicking ability that gained him the nickname of "Superfoot." In the seminars that he has taught around the world, Bill spends a great deal of time explaining this theory. For years, Bill has lifted his left leg into the same lead kicking position. From this one position, he was able to side kick to the head or body, hook kick to the head or groin and wheel kick to the head. He could throw a variety of combinations using these same kicks. From one lead kicking position, Bill developed five angles of attack. Every opponent that ever stepped into the ring with Mr. Wallace, whether it was in semi-contact or full-contact competition, knew that, because of his injured right knee, Bill could only kick with his left leg. His ability to change his angle of attack and deliver his combinations from this one lead position, plus many other skills, allowed Bill to retire as the undefeated Middle Weight Champion of the World. Let us examine a number of these combinations that may be used from a good lead kicking position. You will notice that all of the lead positions used in this chapter place the weapon between the attacker and his opponent, even when they are being used as a set-up for the combination. This concept must always be followed. Remember that, when you start your attack, you can never be positive how the defender is going to react. If your lead technique does not place a weapon between the two of you, and the defender attacks at the same time you do, you will find yourself in the kind of awkward situation we illustrated in the last chapter.

Front Kick

To study the theory of combinations from a lead technique, we must first start with a lead technique. In this illustration, we will be using a simple lead front kick. If you will study the photos, you will see the lead position that you must achieve in order to throw the various combinations we will demonstrate. Notice that the knee is positioned high with the toes pulled back and ready to kick. This puts the weapon between you and your opponent.

The first option that you will always have with a lead technique is to throw the first kick. As you see in this sequence of pictures, the defender has not reacted to my lead movement. Because he has not made any defensive change, I can continue with my original technique. For the follow-up, I use a left reverse punch to the head to keep the opponent on the defensive. Remember, that only one out of five lead techniques will actually score a point. For this reason, it is important to train yourself to follow-up with additional techniques.

Fighting stance.

Attack begins.

Front kick.

Reverse punch.

Fake Front Kick — Wheel Kick — Backhand — Reverse Punch

As the attack gets under way, you will see that the offensive fighter has moved into the proper lead kicking position. At this point, the defender is starting a down block with his left arm in an attempt to deflect an anticipated kick. The photos show that this defensive action has left the defender's head open for attack. At this point, the attacker lifts his hip into a wheel kick position thereby changing his angle of attack in relation to this new opening. Once the attacker executes his wheel kick, he follows up with a quick backhand to the head, followed by a reverse punch to the body. Always remember to follow up your attack. Just because you have created an opening, you should never assume that your next technique will be the one that scores.

Fighting stance.

Beginning front kick.

Changing the angle of attack.

Wheel kick to the head.

Backhand to the head.

Reverse punch.

Fake Front Kick – Lunge Punch – Sweep – Reverse Punch – Inverted Punch

The beginning of this attack is identical to our last illustration. I have led with my front kick and the opponent is trying to defend himself with a down block. For those students that do not have the stretching ability or speed to kick to the head effectively, they can follow-up by continuing to drive forward from this lead movement with a lunge punch to the head. Look at the photos and you will see that, as I deliver the punch to the head, I step to the outside of my opponent's lead leg with my lead leg. This is a crucial position in order to maintain physical control over your opponent. With my foot to the outside of the defender's lead leg, I execute a foot sweep with my lead leg to break my opponent's balance. With the defender turned by the sweep, I continue my attack with a reverse punch to the head, followed by an inverted punch to the body. It should be pointed out that once you have taken your opponent off balance with a foot sweep, you should try, as I have in the photos, to never let your opponent regain his balance and return to a good fighting stance.

Fighting stance.

Faking the front kick.

Lunge punch.

Foot sweep.

Reverse punch.

Inverted punch.

Fake Front Kick — Hook Kick — Wheel Kick

For the advanced student, here is an excellent kicking combination that takes a great deal of skill to execute. As the combination begins, you will notice that the offensive fighter changes his angle of attack to the outside as shown in the photos. The attack is taken to the outside because, when you are in a horse stance, you will find that you have limited vision to the outside over your lead shoulder. This limited vision creates a blind spot and makes it more difficult to defend against techniques being thrown from this angle. In the next photo, the hook kick has been delivered and the leg is cocked and ready to kick again. At this point in the combination, it is critical to keep your leg in the same high position that we have illustrated. Most beginning students will have a tendency to drop their leg after the execution of the hook kick making it impossible to throw the second kick. The proper execution of this combination is from the high finish of the hook kick . The attacker snaps his leg forward and executes a wheel kick to the opposite side of his opponent's face. Although this is a very difficult technique, it is the same type of combination that made Bill Wallace a superb fighter. Practice this combination and you will add another dynamic attack to your arsenal.

Fighting stance.

Faking the front kick.

Changing the angle of attack.

Hook kick to the head.

Reset leg.

Wheel kick to the head.

Skipping Back Kick

For those of you that have been studying the martial arts for a long period of time, this lead move should look very familiar. For those students that are new to the art, it is a movement that you should learn as soon as possible. This is the lead move that Bill Wallace used often. It is the lead position that you see in the photos from which we will be executing our combinations. Notice that the knee is in a high position and my heel is pointing at my opponent. This puts the weapon between the defender and myself and makes it very difficult for my opponent to counter. Remember the purpose of this chapter. We are trying to develop a limited number of lead techniques from which we can throw a variety of combinations. The point you must remember is that, if your opponent does not respond to your lead movement, you can continue with your original attack as illustrated.

Fighting stance.

Attack begins.

Setting the leg for the kick.

Skipping back kick.

Skipping Back Kick — Hook Kick — Wheel Kick — Backhand

This combination illustrates how you can take a simple lead technique and convert it into a devastating combination. Once the lead movement is set into motion, it is important to watch for the reaction of the opponent. In the photos, you will see that the defender is dropping his arm to block the anticipated kick to the body. This defensive motion now creates an opening to the head which allows the attacker to bring his leg to the outside and execute a hook kick. In this combination, allow the leg to start dropping to the floor after executing the hook kick to the head. As the kicking leg is dropping to the floor, the attacker follows up with a wheel kick to the groin. At this point, as the attacker, you have already created an opening on your opponent with a good lead technique and then scored with two rapid kicks to the head and groin. You will notice in the illustration that, as you execute the wheel kick to the groin, the defender begins to drop his hands in an effort to defend himself against this technique. This defensive position will once again leave his head open for attack. With the right side forward, you will find that a backhand to the head using the right hand will be your most efficient follow-up technique. This is a combination that I recommend all students to learn. Not only does it demonstrate how effective you can be when you create an opening from a good lead technique, but, in my opinion, it illustrates the beauty and power of the martial arts.

Fighting stance.

Lead position.

Hook kick to the head.

Follow through.

Wheel kick to the groin.

Backhand to the head.

Fake Skipping Back Kick — Reverse Leg Takedown

This technique is quite a bit easier to execute than the last kicking combination. But often, you will find that the easier, more direct attacks, yield the best results. If you are a beginner in the art, these are the type of combinations that you should be practicing most of the time. That is not to say that you shouldn't try to develop higher skills but, as a beginner, and even as an advanced practitioner, these basic combinations should be your "bread and butter" techniques.

In this combination, we again use a skipping back kick to set up the opponent. Once the defender has reacted to your lead technique, you simply continue your forward momentum and step behind the defender's lead leg. Once you are in this position, you must react quickly by kicking your opponent's legs out and taking him to the floor. A common mistake for a beginner is to hesitate once they have stepped behind the defender's lead leg. The problem is that, if you hesitate, your opponent will have the opportunity to take you off your own feet. As we have demonstrated in the photos, once you take a fighter off of his feet, you must learn to follow-up immediately.

Fighting stance.

Attacker advances.

Sets leg for the kick.

Steps behind the lead leg.

Reverse leg takedown.

Follow-up.

Fake Skipping Back Kick — Wheel Kick

This technique is also a basic combination that the beginner should practice. The advanced student should refine this movement for his freestyle fighting. The important transition in this combination is illustrated in the photos. Once the defender has reacted to your lead movement, you must quickly reposition your leg to set it up for your wheel kick. To accomplish this, you must drive your knee forward to point straight at your opponent with the leg cocked and ready to kick. To complete the combination, you simply need to extend your wheel kick to the opponent's head. For those students that look at this combination and feel it is too basic, you should be reminded once again that Bill Wallace has scored with this same combination hundreds of times in his career. For the karate practitioner, it is crucial to develop strong basics. Remember that if your basic moves are weak or sloppy, it will be impossible for you to develop any of the advanced combinations.

Let us review the contents of this chapter. The first thing to remember is that you should develop your combinations from good lead techniques. You can never be sure what the reaction of your opponent will be when you start your attack. By always keeping a weapon between the two of you when you start your attack, you will make it very difficult for the defender to counter attack. The next thing to remember is that once you have moved into your lead position, you want to develop a variety of techniques and combinations that you can throw from this one position. This gives us the ability to change our angle of attack as our opponent changes his angle of defense. Finally, learn to develop explosive combinations from these lead techniques. If you continue to assume that your lead technique will always score on your opponent, you will find that you can never develop a strong offensive attack. You will gain minimal results as an offensive fighter.

Fighting stance.

Faking skipping back kick.

Changing angle of attack.

Wheel kick to the head.

Three crucial points for good fighting combinations.

1. Develop combinations from good lead techniques.

2. Develop many combinations and varieties of attack from your basic lead position.

3. Develop explosive combinations from your lead attack.

CHAPTER IV

COMBINATIONS FROM LEAD TECHNIQUES (HANDS)

In the last chapter, we concentrated on combinations that commenced with a lead kicking motion. In this chapter, we will deal with lead techniques with the hands and the different combinations you can deliver from these lead moves. You will find that, by using a hand technique for a lead movement, you will increase the speed of your attack. This will be especially helpful when attacking an opponent who retreats quickly.

The first thing that you will discover, when trying to attack an opponent who always retreats, is that it is very difficult to hit him with kicking combinations. The reason for this is quite simple. Once you have raised one of your legs to kick, it becomes almost impossible to maintain the high level of speed needed in your attack to catch your opponent. If you doubt this statement, I would like you to conduct the following test the next time in class. Square off with a partner and tell him what you need to practice. Inform him that you are going to attack him with a three part kicking combination and all you want him to do is to maintain enough distance so none of your kicks will score. In order to make this test valid, you must attack as quickly as possible and make an honest attempt to score one of the three kicks. Try this at least ten times with the same partner. If you hit him twice in the ten attacks give yourself a gold star and tell your partner to take up bowling. What you will probably find is that your opponent is easily able to avoid your attack. The second problem in throwing a series of kicks at your opponent is that you create gaps in the timing of your attack. The gaps are caused by the extra time needed to deliver a series of kicks as compared to the same number of punches. These gaps between kicks gives the defender extra time in which to counter your attack. The reason that Bill Wallace was so successful with his kicking combinations is that he used these techniques when his opponent was trying to create distance and then counter his lead move. Don't confuse this type of fighter with the one who only moves back for the purpose of avoiding your attack and has no thought of countering.

The adjustment that you need to make against this type of fighter is in the hands. The most effective attack against a retreating fighter is explosive hand combinations. If you remember the results of our experiment in the previous chapter, students attacking with three part hand combinations scored on their opponent ninety percent of the time. This percentage should be quite a bit higher than the results you achieved with a three part kicking combination. The other advantage of developing explosive hand combinations lies in the speed of the attack. Because of the speed of hand combinations, it becomes increasingly difficult for your opponent to score on you with a counter attack. Although it will still be possible for your opponent to score, you will find that the more explosive you become in your attack, the more pressure you will put on the defender to counter with more exact timing.

In this chapter, we will examine a variety of hand combinations that can be used by the offensive fighter. You will notice that, in a few of the combinations, we will be finishing the attack with a kick. This would seem to contradict what I just told you, although it really does not. We do not throw the kick at our opponent until we have closed the distance with our hand techniques. As stated earlier, once you have closed the distance on your opponent, you may choose from a wide variety of techniques to continue your attack. This chapter is only to help you select techniques to close this distance between yourself and the other fighter.

Like all good lead techniques, we will try to accomplish three objectives when leading with the hands. First, we must select a technique that will close the distance on the opponent quickly. Secondly, we will select a technique that will put a weapon between us and the opponent. Finally, we will want to select a lead technique that will allow us to change our angle of attack as the opponent sets up his defense. Let us now look at these lead hand techniques.

Backhand

The backhand is one of the best techniques for a beginner to learn. It can be used to teach how to close the distance quickly and throw effective combinations. This technique can be delivered quickly and puts the weapon between yourself and your opponent. A point that I have illustrated here, as discussed earlier, is that the most effective lead techniques are the ones in which the weapon moves first. Often the attacker will move his body before the technique is started. This early movement will often give the defender the extra time needed to retreat from the attack. What you will find through practice is that, if you give your opponent this extra head start, it becomes almost impossible to close the distance and score with any of your combinations. It therefore becomes crucial that you learn, as illustrated, to start the movement of your technique first, and then let your body close the distance. By learning to throw a good lead technique, you will improve your ability to throw good combinations.

Fighting stance.

Hand begins to move first.

Body moves.

Backhand scores.

Backhand - Footsweep - Reverse Punch

One of my favorite techniques over the years has been the foot sweep. It is the best way possible to destroy the retreat of your opponent and is one of the few techniques that, if executed properly, can put you in complete control of the other fighter. In this series of photos, I will demonstrate how to use a lead backhand to set the defender up for this technique. The first thing that you should notice is that I have changed my foot movement in order to close the distance. Instead of keeping my right foot forward when the attack is started, I step across with my left foot to close the distance on my opponent while throwing my lead backhand at the same time. Once I have taken this step and the defender begins to retreat, I attack his front leg with a foot sweep. You will find that the foot sweep will give you the best results if you learn to attack your opponent's leg while it is moving. It is when the fighter's weight is shifting from one leg to the other that they can be swept with a minimum of effort on your part. Once my opponent has been turned out of position, I continue my attack with a reverse punch to the head.

Fighting stance.

Lead backhand.

Foot sweep.

Follow-up reverse punch.

Backhand - Reverse Punch - Wheel Kick

To close the distance in this technique, I again step through with my rear leg. The importance of taking this step is that it creates a counter-balance that will allow me to continue my attack at a quicker speed. What I mean when I say that I create a counter-balance can be demonstrated by, for example, simply going for a short walk. Stand up and take a few steps forward. That is probably very easy for you to do. Now do the same test again, except this time, swing your left arm forward when you step with your left foot, and swing the right arm forward when you advance with the right foot. Did it feel awkward? Even in walking, we counter-balance ourselves by swinging the opposite arm forward when we take a step. For example, when we step with the right foot, we swing the left arm forward. If you wish to develop explosive hand techniques, it is crucial that you learn to counter-balance yourself in this manner when attacking. In this sequence of photos, you will notice that I counter-balance myself with my first two techniques. With both my backhand and the reverse punch, I have stepped with the opposite foot to the hand that is punching. Once I close the distance on the defender, I can now use a kicking technique. Here, I have chosen a wheel kick to conclude the attack.

Fighting stance.

Step across backhand.

Step across reverse punch.

Wheel kick.

Step Across Reverse Punch

Although a step across reverse punch and a backhand may look like similar lead techniques, they are not. The difference is in the line of attack. The reverse punch is being delivered on a straight line to the target, while the backhand is thrown at a slight angle. This change in the angle of attack will change the defender's angle of defense. This concept will be discussed in greater detail in the next chapter.

This lead technique is similar to all of the other lead techniques we have discussed. The weapon will move first and be placed immediately between the attacker and the defender. An important factor in this lead movement is the timing. As my advancing leg begins to set, my punch should be making its contact. This timing will help to maximize the velocity of your punch and greatly increase the power of your technique. The step across reverse punch is an excellent lead technique. It allows you to close the distance quickly on your opponent and gives you the freedom to select from a wide variety of follow-up techniques.

Fighting stance.

Weapon begins to move.

Body starts to close the distance.

Step across reverse punch.

Reverse Punch - Reverse Punch - Front Kick

Remember the objective of this chapter. We are trying to close the distance on our opponent as quickly as possible. At the same time, we are trying to deliver our own techniques at a speed that will leave few, if any, gaps in which the defender can execute a counter attack.

This simple three part combination fulfills all of these objectives. Once the first step has been taken and the opponent begins to retreat, I follow up immediately by taking another step forward and throwing a second reverse punch. These two steps executed at full speed will help me to close the distance quickly on the defender. As we discussed in the last chapter, it should be impossible for your opponent to move backwards as fast as you can move forwards. If you find that the defender is able to maintain his distance during your attack, you must reexamine your lead motion. Make sure you are not giving your attack away by an early movement. This mistake can give your opponent enough of a defensive headstart to avoid your attack. Once I have closed to within punching range of my opponent, I will use my arms like a ruler. In this series of photos, as I throw my second punch, I realize that I am just out of reach of the defender. I then select a front kick for my third technique. The use of my legs at this time will give me the added reach necessary to close the distance on the defender and score.

Fighting stance.

Lead reverse punch.

Follow-up reverse punch.

Front kick.

Reverse Punch - Reverse Punch - Reverse Leg Takedown

In this series of photos, we will change the situation by putting the defender in a horse stance. The lead move of the two reverse punches will remain exactly the same as the last example we studied. We have mentioned on several occasions that once you close the distance, you may use a number of different techniques to complete your combination. In this situation, I will try to take advantage of the fact that my opponent has selected a horse stance. Once I have closed the distance I immediately move to the outside of the defender's front leg. Moving into this position gives me the opportunity to take physical control of the other fighter. Once I have set behind the lead leg, I quickly execute my reverse leg takedown before my opponent can counter me with a throw of his own. As the defender falls to the floor, I finish my technique with a side kick to the head. I have always favored the use of takedowns in my freestyle fighting. The ability to take your opponent off of his feet demonstrates total control over your partner.

Fighting stance.

Left reverse punch.

Right reverse punch.

Step behind lead leg.

Reverse leg takedown.

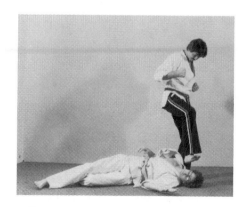

Follow-up.

Reverse Punch - Backhand - Reverse Punch

In this example, I will demonstrate a combination that can be used when you have closed the distance on your opponent sooner than you expected. Often when this happens, the attacker will find that the timing of his second technique is off and his body closes the distance faster then he can throw another punch. What is needed in this type of situation is a technique that can be thrown in rapid succession to the lead move. This series of photos shows that the attacker has reached the opponent with his lead technique and the defender has been forced to block. At this point, I quickly roll my lead hand over and execute a backhand to the head before the defender can start his counter. (Examine the inserts to understand how this technique is executed.) This move allows me to keep my momentum going forward and gives me the opportunity to continue with my combination. Because I have already closed the distance, it is not necessary for me to take any more steps forward. I therefore conclude my combination with a quick reverse punch.

In the last two chapters, we have studied a variety of combinations that can be thrown from your lead technique with both hands and feet. These are only a few of the possibilities that exist. Take the time to practice and develop some combinations that feel comfortable to you. When developing these combinations just remember to follow these two simple rules.

Rule 1. When selecting a lead move, make sure to select a technique that:
  a) Will close the distance on your opponent quickly.
  b) Puts the weapon between yourself and the opponent.
  c) Will create an opening on your opponent or get them to move into a weaker fighting stance.

Rule 2. Once you have moved into your lead position, develop a variety of techniques that will allow you to change your angle of attack and continue your combination to score.

Fighting stance.

Right reverse punch.

Rolls right lead hand.

Right backhand to the head.

Follow-up reverse punch.

a. Block.

b. The right hand rolls off the defender's block.

c. Immediately step following through with a second backhand.

d. This move can also alternate as a block against his attack.

If you are a new student, I would suggest that you select two simple techniques and then develop three combinations for each of these opening moves. This will give you six different attacks to practice. As you perfect these combinations, you can then expand your attack techniques by developing other lead techniques and combinations. Remember to keep it simple. You'll find that a well placed front kick is just as effective as a spinning heel kick. Keep the combinations within your ability. Practice your basics and your combinations will naturally improve.

CHAPTER V

DEFENSIVE THEORIES

Up to this point, I have dedicated a large majority of this book to the explanation and illustration of effective offensive techniques. What about the person who is on the other end of these punches and kicks? The point is that there are two sides to every coin. And now that we have spent so much time on the offensive side of the art, I think it is time we discussed the defensive aspects in some detail.

The development of good defensive techniques is crucial to the growth of every martial artist. Not only do these defensive techniques protect you from the attacks of your opponent, but as you will find in this chapter, an effective block will completely stop your opponent's attack and give you the opportunity to counter-attack with a technique of your own.

In watching thousands of students in competition over the years, I have noticed that only a small percentage of these fighters have developed good defensive movements and blocks. The building of a strong defense is not accidental. It takes a great deal of practice of the physical movements as well as a complete understanding of the theories that make these techniques so effective. That's right! There are theories to defensive fighting just like there are theories for good offensive fighting. Remember that, as a martial artist, every movement must have meaning and purpose. Let us first examine these various theories and then we will give you some examples of how these theories can be applied in combative situations.

The first concern in developing an effective defense must be the stance. In the first chapter, we discussed the strengths and weaknesses of the most common fighting stances, so I will not be repeating that portion in this chapter. However, I must remind you that the fighting stance you select will play an important role in your ability to defend yourself. My suggestion is to develop two or three different stances that you can use effectively. This will give you the flexibility to adjust to your opponent's style of fighting. Once a stance has been selected, you must then spend a great deal of time practicing how to retreat properly from this stance. No matter how aggressive a fighter you think you are, there will always come a time when you are required to move away from your opponent's attack. The theory is that you want to move backwards fast enough to avoid being struck by your opponent's attack, but at the same time, maintain a strong stance so you can throw your counter-attack with power. Remember, if the attacker can get you to retreat in such a fashion that you end up in a weak fighting stance, he has gained the advantage on you. Watch students at all levels of training while they are freestyle fighting, and you will see a countless number of examples of how moving into a weak stance can get yourself into trouble. If you believe that your stance is good enough to use when you start the match, then you should want to stay in that stance for the entire fight. This is not to say that you can't change into another stance during a match, but be sure you are in a good stance. Often, while moving about the floor, students will get their feet in a position that resembles none of the stances that have been taught and that is when they find themselves in big trouble.

Once you have learned how to move in your stance, the next question you must ask yourself is, "how far back should I move?" The ability to distance properly is, by far, the most important of the three theories we will discuss in this chapter. Not only will proper distancing keep you out of the range of your opponent's attack, but it should place you in the proper position to execute your own counter attack. This position represents a very fine line. If you are a few inches too close you may be hit by your opponent's attack. And, if you have moved back a few inches too far, you will be out of position to score with your counter technique. You will also find that the height of your opponent will change the distance you will need to retreat in order to find this spot. Let me give the definition of my distancing theory and see if this will help you to better understand this concept. When attacked, the defender must move back far enough so that, if your block misses, so does the attack while, at the same time, staying close enough to your opponent to counter effectively. Study the next three illustrations and you will see how this theory can be applied.

Improper Distancing (too close)

This illustration represents one of the most commonly made mistakes by both beginning and advanced students. They become so preoccupied with blocking the attack that they forget to set the proper distance between themselves and the attacker. In this sequence of photos, you will see just this type of mistake. As the attacker begins to lead with his front kick, the defender makes no effort to move backwards, but tries to deflect the kick with a down-block. Once the attacker sees this reaction, he changes his angle of attack and throws a wheel-kick to the head. The defender has been caught off guard and, because he has not adjusted his distancing to the first attack, the wheel-kick will score. Had the defender set the proper distance on the first attack, the result would have been different. He still would have missed the initial attack with his down-block, but the wheel-kick to the head would have also missed and the defender would still be in a position to counter-attack.

Fighting stance.

Faking front kick—defender too close.

Changing angle of attack.

Defender struck by the heel kick.

Improper Distancing (too far)

The other common mistake that is made by students is that they move back too far when the first attack is thrown. In this illustration, you will see that, as the attacker throws the lead front-kick, the defender moves back a great distance. When the attacker continues with his combination and throws the wheel-kick to the head, this technique is also short of the target. The fact that the second technique also missed the defender is good, because the defender has been able to avoid both attacks. But as you can see in the illustration, when the defender tries to score with his counter technique, he is also short of the target. So, in this case, the extra distance kept the defender from being hit, but it has also prevented the defender from striking and countering against his opponent.

Fighting stance.

Faking front kick—defender too far away.

Wheel kick short of the target.

Counter short of the target.

Proper Distancing

In the last two illustrations, we have seen some of the more common distancing mistakes made by students. Now let us take a look at an illustration of the result we are trying to achieve with the theory of proper distancing. When the attack begins, you will notice that while the defender is executing a down-block he is also moving back slightly to avoid the kick. Notice that, even with this backward movement, the defender still maintains a strong fighting stance. As the attacker changes his angle of attack and throws the wheel-kick to the head, he does, in fact, catch the defender off guard. (You will notice that the defender's block is still down leaving his head open for attack.) Because of the defender's distancing of the first technique, the second kick also misses. This goes along with the distancing theory that if the block misses, so does the technique. Once the second technique is thrown, the defender has the opportunity to react with a counter. The last phase of this sequence not only shows the technique being used for this counter, but also illustrates the fact that I have turned my defensive position into one of offense and control.

Hopefully, these three illustrations have helped you to understand the theory of distancing. This theory is an important element of good defensive fighting and should be studied closely.

The final theory of good defensive fighting is that you should think of your block as an offensive weapon. Many students only think of their blocks as a way to prevent the attacker from scoring a point. But a well executed block can be much more than just a vehicle of defense, it can be a weapon of its own. In my opinion, a well executed block should have three major objectives. First, it should prevent the attacker from hitting you. Secondly, the block should remove the attacking weapon between you and your opponent. This will give you a straight line of attack for your counter and you will not have to worry about the attacker throwing a second kick. Third, a good block should take your opponent off balance in such a fashion that they will not be able to continue with their attack or counter. The reason that many blocks used do not achieve these results is that the students are smothering the attack rather then blocking the attack. Let us look at some illustrations that will show you the difference between smothering an attack and blocking it.

Fighting stance.

Faking front kick—defender moves back the proper distance.

Block misses—wheel kick short of the target.

Defender scores with the counter.

Smothering (improper block)

The problem with smothering a kick rather than blocking it is clearly demonstrated in this series of photos. As you can see, when the kick is thrown, the defender smothers the attack by executing a down-block with his arm at a right angle to the attacker's kick. This means that the defender will be taking the full force of the kick on his arm. You only need to look at the difference in size between your own arm and leg to see what a mismatch is created. The other problem created by this type of blocking is that, after the kick has been smothered by the defender's arm, the attacker will be allowed to pull his leg back on a straight line. When the defender is allowed to return to this position, he will still have the momentum needed to continue the attack. So as we have illustrated in this sequence of photos, the fact that the first technique has been stopped does not mean that you have stopped the entire attack.

Fighting stance.

Front kick smothered.

Attacker's momentum continues forward.

Lunge punch to the head.

Smothering (improper block)

Another problem you will encounter when you smother a lead kick is that you have not moved the opponent's weapon away from yourself. In this illustration, you will see the type of problem this can create when you don't move the weapon (foot) out of the way. As the attacker retracts his leg, the defender starts his counter-attack. As you can see in the photos, the attacker has still been left with a clear line of attack at the defender. The offensive fighter merely needs to repeat the same front kick a second time, and as you see here, the defender runs right into the technique. As the defender, you are not ready to counter until you have cleared the area between yourself and your opponent, giving yourself an unobstructed line of attack.

Fighting stance.

Defender smothers kick.

Attacker retracts leg to good lead position.

Attacker scores with a second front kick.

Proper Blocking

Now that we have seen the trouble we can get into when we block improperly, let us take a look at an example of what we can achieve defensively with a well executed down-block. As in the last two examples, the attacker is leading with a straight front kick. You will notice in this series of pictures that the blocking arm has struck my opponent's leg at the side of the ankle. This angle creates a deflection and will eliminate a large amount of the shock your arm receives when smothering a kick. As I continue my blocking motion, you will see that I have moved my opponent's weapon away from my body. Now that the weapon is no longer between the two of us, I am ready to start my counter-attack. As my opponent's momentum continues forward, you will see the second effect of a good block. By the time his foot gets back to the floor, he has been spun into such an awkward position that it is almost impossible for him to defend himself. At this point, it is simply a matter of executing my counter to score the point.

Although not every block will yield this type of an advantage, it should always be your goal to try and put your opponent in this type of position when you block.

The third theory of blocking has to do with the concept of turning your opponent. The theory, itself, is very simple. When blocking, always turn your opponent to the outside. As we have just stated, one of the objectives of a good block is to turn your opponent. You will find, however, that if you don't turn your opponent to the outside, you will create additional problems for yourself. I think I can best illustrate the reason for this theory with one simple example.

Fighting stance.

Defender blocking kick properly.

Attacker being turned away.

Defender in control and countering.

Improper Block (turning inside)

This sequence of pictures should make it clear why you always want to turn the attacker to the outside. In this situation, the defender has done just the opposite. Although he has executed his block properly, he has turned his opponent to the inside. When you block this way, you are, in fact, turning your attacker's hips into you. This inward rotation will often increase the power in the defender's second technique. Even though the defender is scoring with a technique to the body, he is taking a solid punch to the head. So, in fact, he has gained no advantage on his opponent at all. And depending on the power of the attacker's reverse punch, he may have lost the war.

This is obviously not the result we are looking for when we block. To practice these theories, pair off with a partner and have him throw a variety of lead techniques. Have him throw techniques that are good lead moves and other techniques that are not good lead techniques. Remember, not everyone you fight will have read this book. Think of all the blocks you can use to turn your partner to the outside. Continue to practice these blocks until they become second-nature to you. To help you along in this exercise, let us take a look at a few more examples of how to block effectively to show you how all the theories we have discussed in this chapter play an important role in this process.

Fighting stance.

Attack begins.

Defender turning attacker inside.

Defender being struck.

Reverse Down Block

As we have just stated, one of the theories of effective blocking is to turn your opponent to the outside. The reverse down block allows you to achieve this objective without switching the position of your feet. In this example, if I were to use a traditional down-block with the front hand, I would be turning the attacker to the inside. Instead, I merely rotate my arm in a counter-clockwise position with the palm of my hand facing outward. As I start this rotation, I will retreat from my opponent's attack to set up the proper distance. During this movement, I will maintain a good fighting stance. When I execute the block I will try to make contact on the outside of my opponent's ankle with the meaty portion of my forearm. I will continue this rotation to a point where I am sure I have cleared the weapon away from myself. At this point, I am ready to counter and score on my opponent with a simple reverse-punch to the body.

Fighting stance.

Reverse down block.

Opponent being turned.

Counter technique.

Defense Against a Backhand

The backhand is one of the hardest techniques to effectively defend against. It is a technique that can be delivered very quickly and allows the attacker to follow up with rapid combinations. To counter this attack, the defender's timing must be perfect. You will see in this series that, as the attacker starts to deliver the backhand, I must start my inside-block immediately. My objective when I execute this block is to block the attacker's arm just as he extends his punch. If you can achieve this, you will find that your block will turn the attacker's lead shoulder to the outside as illustrated. By turning your opponent's shoulder in this fashion, you will take away his ability to continue with the attack. At this point, you must execute your counter immediately. Because of your opponent's arm position, I would suggest you counter with a reverse-punch to the ribs.

Fighting stance.

Lead backhand.

Defender turning opponent.

Counter reverse punch.

Counter to the Wheel-Kick

This counter is one of the most spectacular defensive moves I have ever seen in our sport. It combines the elements of timing, speed, and strength, and if properly executed, can have a devastating effect on your opponent. Although the wheel-kick is not a good lead technique, it is often used. When the kick is delivered, you must first make sure that your block stops the attack. At the point of contact with the blocking arm, we try to trap the kicking leg by lifting our left arm into the position demonstrated. This method of trapping prevents the opponent from throwing a second kick to the head with the same leg. From here, we slide forward and set our lead leg behind the opponent's rear leg. At the same time, you must also grab the lead shoulder of the attacker to prevent him from trying to throw a technique with this hand. Once you have accomplished this, lift the opponent and kick his leg out from under. After he has been taken off his feet, you can execute a variety of follow-up techniques. In this illustration, I have used a punch to the stomach. It must be stressed that this technique can be extremely dangerous. When practicing this move, you must continue to hold on to your opponent's shoulder during the throw to prevent his head from striking the floor.

Fighting stance.

Lead wheel kick and block.

Trapping the leg.

Defender setting behind the rear leg.

Throw.

Lift.

Follow-up technique.

Counter to the Reverse-Punch

In this series of photos, you will be learning a skill called off-hand blocking. This technique is rarely used in competition, but with practice, you will find that the use of this block will greatly increase the speed of your counter. As the attacker moves in with his reverse punch, I move back slightly to escape the power of this technique. As you can see, I have maintained my fighting stance in order to counter effectively. As the punch is delivered, I execute an off-hand down-block with my right hand. The norm in this type of situation would be to block with the front hand. Once the block is executed and I have turned my opponent, I throw a front hand punch to stop the attacker's charge. For purposes of illustration, we have shown the block and counter as two separate photos. In reality, these two techniques should be delivered simultaneously. By using this timing, you will find that your counters are much faster. Your attacker will have a difficult time in defending himself against these moves.

In this chapter, we have discussed several different theories that I feel are crucial in developing a solid defense. Let us take just a few minutes to review these theories.

The first concern of a fighter must be his stance. When talking about defensive fighting, the stance plays an important role. It is crucial that you stay in a strong fighting stance as you retreat. You will find that if you move into a weak stance as you retreat, your attacker will have gained an important advantage over you. Take the time to practice staying in a strong stance and I'm sure that you will find that this will hinder your opponent's ability to gain the advantage over you.

The second theory was distancing. The ideal position to achieve when moving back is one that is just out of reach of your attacker's lead technique. Remember the goal, if the block misses so does the technique. But don't move back too far or you will not be in a position to counter attack. This concept will take a lot of practice. Be patient and let time and training take their course.

Finally, we defined my blocking theory. Think of your block as a weapon. The ideal block will always clear the weapon from between the opponent and yourself. In doing this, I want to turn my attacker to the outside in such a fashion that he will be unable to continue with his attack or counter-attack. This is a concept that every student must learn immediately. Learn this theory and you will see vast improvements in your defensive ability.

These are the skills that you must develop in order to become a good defensive fighter. Learning these skills at a high level of efficiency will take most of you a great deal of time. But remember that time is all we have. The important thing is how we spend it.

Fighting stance.

Lead reverse punch.

Off-hand block.

Front hand strike to the face.

The three important elements of defensive fighting.

1. Finding a good stance and learning how to retreat effectively and properly without sacrificing your balance.

2. Knowing how far to move back to dissolve the attack yet be in a position to execute your own moves against your opponent.

3. Thinking of your blocks and defensive moves as offensive techniques.

An effective block achieves three purposes:

1. Prevents or stops the opponent's attack.

2. Removes the weapon (attacker's hand or foot) out of the line of fire.

3. Throws the opponent off balance so he cannot continue his attack. You must turn your opponent away from yourself.

Closing

I couldn't end this book without taking the time to thank my first instructor in karate, Mr. Rodney Hu. It was his patience and love of the art that instilled in me the spirit to train all of these years. Without him, this book would never have been written.

I would also like to thank the thousands of students that I have trained in the past fourteen years. You have made the years seem like days and you have taught me a great deal about the art and myself.